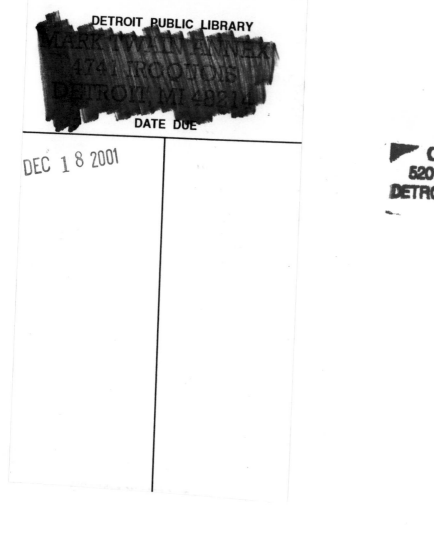

TIGERS

BY SUSAN SCHAFER

BENCHMARK **B**OOKS

MARSHALL CAVENDISH
NEW YORK

With thanks to Paul Severtson; Brooke Love; Naresh, Deepika, and Neelie Jaggi; Phil and Carla Wingenbach

Series Consultant: James Doherty
General Curator
Bronx Zoo, New York

Benchmark Books
Marshall Cavendish Corporation
99 White Plains Road
Tarrytown, NY 10591-9001

Library of Congress Cataloging-in-Publication data:
Schafer, Susan.
Tigers / by Susan Schafer.
p. cm. – (Animals, animals)
Includes index (p. 48)
Summary: Describes the physical characteristics, behavior, habitat, and endangered status of tigers.
ISBN 0-7614-1170-4
1. Tigers–Juvenile literature. [1. Tigers. 2. Endangered species.] I. Title. II. Series.
QL737.C23   S289   2000
599.756–dc21   00-027311

Cover photo: *Animals, Animals* / Zig Leszczynski

All photographs are used by permission and through the courtesy of *Animals, Animals*: Zig Leszczynski: 4, 27, 28, 32 (right), 34; A. & M. Shah: 7, 24 (right); Alfred B. Thomas: 8; Ralph Reinhold: 10; Dani/Jeske: 13, 37, 41 (top & bottom), 42; John Chelman: 14; Anup Shah: 15, 16, 24 (left), 25, 43; Peter Weimann: 19, 20; Robert Winslow: 21; Joe McDonald: 23, 32 (left); M. Singh: 31; Lynn M. Stone: 36 (inset); E. R. Degginger: 39.

Printed in the United States

1 3 5 6 4 2

CONTENTS

1
INTRODUCING TIGERS

Tigers are fierce hunters. They prowl the forest at night, pouncing on their *prey* in a burst of power and speed. It's no wonder that people have always looked at the tiger with a mixture of fear and fascination.

Tigers belong to the cat family. They are the largest *species* of cat and the largest *predator* on land. Their closest relatives are the jaguar, leopard, snow leopard, and lion. Five special kinds, or *subspecies*, of tigers live in the world today: the Bengal tiger in and around India, the Siberian tiger in China and Russia, the Indochinese tiger in southeast Asia, the South China tiger, and the Sumatran tiger.

Think of tigers and you think of stripes. A tiger's stripes are like your fingerprints: no two tigers have the same pattern. Beneath their red-orange fur, their massive

A BENGAL TIGER'S GROWL SHOWS OFF ITS IMPRESSIVE TEETH.

bodies bulge with muscles. Their footprints can be five by six inches (13 by 15 centimeters) and would dwarf your hand if you placed it inside.

Male and female tigers look alike, but males are larger and have longer whiskers. Older males also have a ruff of fur around their necks. Depending on the sub–species, males may be nine feet (3 meters) long, not counting the tail. That's longer than a standard truck bed. Females are about a foot shorter. Males weigh about 400 pounds (180 kilograms), more than two big men together. Females, at about 250 pounds (113 kg), are considerably lighter.

The tiger, lion, leopard, jaguar, and snow leopard belong to a group of cats called the "big cats." Yet each is unique in its own way. The tiger is the largest. The leopard has the widest range, covering Asia and Africa. The jaguar is the most powerful. The lion is the only cat that lives in a pride, or group, and has a mane. The snow leopard is the only cat that lives high in the mountains above the tree line.

A BENGAL TIGER YAWNS AFTER A LONG DAY OF HUNTING.

. . .

THE SABER-TOOTHED TIGER ONCE ROAMED THE EARTH, PREYING ON LARGE PLANT-EATING MAMMALS LIKE THE MASTODON. ITS UPPER CANINE TEETH— NEARLY 8 INCHES (20 CM) LONG—SLASHED LIKE KNIFE BLADES. WHILE JUST AS SHARP, THE CANINES OF TODAY'S TIGERS ARE ONLY UP TO 3 INCHES (8 CM) LONG. SABER-TOOTHED TIGERS ARE NOT THE ANCESTORS OF MODERN TIGERS. THEY BELONGED TO A SEPARATE BRANCH OF THE CAT FAMILY THAT DIED OUT THOUSANDS OF YEARS AGO.

. . .

THESE BENGAL TIGERS ARE BROTHER AND SISTER.

. . .

HONORED THROUGHOUT CHINA FOR ITS STRENGTH, THE TIGER IS ONE OF THE TWELVE ANIMALS CELEBRATED IN THE SIXTY-YEAR CHINESE CALENDAR. THE MARKINGS ON ITS FOREHEAD LOOK LIKE THE CHINESE SYMBOL WANG, WHICH MEANS "KING." CHILDREN BORN DURING THE YEAR OF THE TIGER ARE BELIEVED TO BE PROTECTED FROM EVIL. TO MAKE SURE A BABY STAYS HEALTHY, TIGERS ARE EMBROIDERED ON THEIR CAPS, SHOES, AND PILLOWS.

. . .

9

SIBERIAN TIGERS LIVE IN COLD CLIMATES. THIS ONE LIVES IN THE HEILONGJIANG TIGER RESERVE IN NORTHERN CHINA.

The farther north tigers live, the larger they are. The largest is the Siberian tiger. It lives in the far north of Russia. Male Siberian tigers may grow to nearly 11 feet (3.5 m) and weigh 675 pounds (303 kg). They need to be larger to withstand the cold. They also have longer, thicker fur to keep them warm.

The smallest tiger is the Sumatran tiger. Male Sumatran tigers are only 8 feet (2.5 m) and weigh about 300 pounds (135 kg). Sumatrans live south in the *tropics*. They need to be smaller to beat the heat.

THE LARGEST TIGER
IS THE SIBERIAN
TIGER. THE
SMALLEST IS THE
SUMATRAN TIGER.

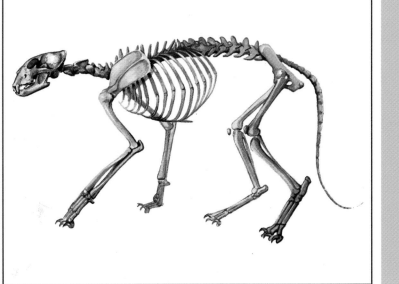

THIS IS A TIGER'S
SKELETON. NOTE THE
TEETH, CLAWS, AND
POWERFUL JAW—
IDEAL TOOLS FOR
KILLING PREY.

2
BLENDING INTO THE FOREST

All tigers live in dense forests. If it weren't for the trees and plants of these forests, the tiger might not be striped. The leaves, vines, branches, and tree trunks cast shadows—just like the stripes on a tiger. With their stripes, tigers blend into the background when they hunt. This is called *camouflage*.

Tigers live in different kinds of forests. The Bengal tiger in southern India, the Indochinese tiger, and the Sumatran tiger live in *tropical* rain forests. Tropical rain forests are hot, dark, and wet. Over a hundred inches

A BENGAL TIGER HIDES IN RAIN-FOREST FOLIAGE.

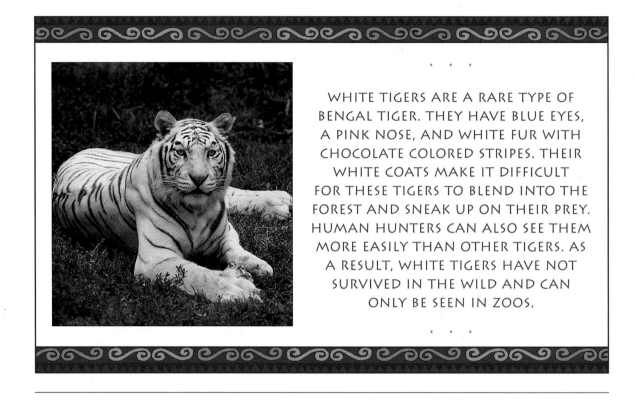

WHITE TIGERS ARE A RARE TYPE OF BENGAL TIGER. THEY HAVE BLUE EYES, A PINK NOSE, AND WHITE FUR WITH CHOCOLATE COLORED STRIPES. THEIR WHITE COATS MAKE IT DIFFICULT FOR THESE TIGERS TO BLEND INTO THE FOREST AND SNEAK UP ON THEIR PREY. HUMAN HUNTERS CAN ALSO SEE THEM MORE EASILY THAN OTHER TIGERS. AS A RESULT, WHITE TIGERS HAVE NOT SURVIVED IN THE WILD AND CAN ONLY BE SEEN IN ZOOS.

(254 cm) of rain fall every year. The trees there are *evergreen*, which means they keep their leaves throughout the year.

The Siberian tiger in China, the Bengal tiger in Nepal, and the South China tiger in southern China live in *deciduous* forests. Deciduous forests are not as hot as rain forests. The trees there—such as oaks and maples—lose their leaves in the fall and grow new ones in the spring.

The Siberian tiger roams the *coniferous* forests of China and Russia. The weather is much colder in these

THE TROPICAL RAIN FOREST IN INDIA IS HOME TO THE BENGAL TIGER.

TIGERS ALSO ROAM THE BORDER AREAS OF
RANTAMBOR NATIONAL PARK IN INDIA.

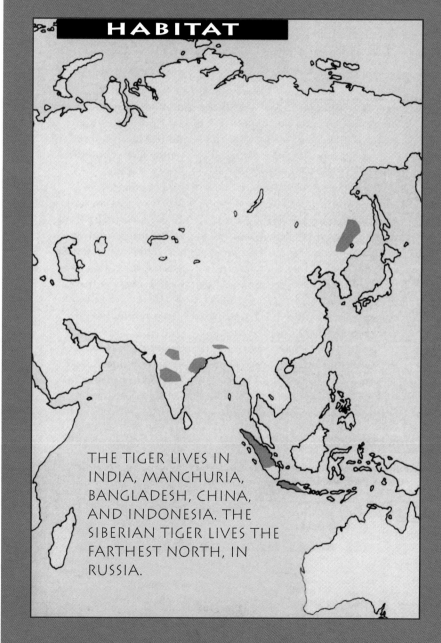

HABITAT

THE TIGER LIVES IN
INDIA, MANCHURIA,
BANGLADESH, CHINA,
AND INDONESIA. THE
SIBERIAN TIGER LIVES THE
FARTHEST NORTH, IN
RUSSIA.

forests. The pine, spruce, and fir trees there have needle–like leaves to withstand winter snows.

Tigers do not live in groups like lions. In the forest it is better if a tiger stalks prey alone. A group might attract too much attention. Tigers usually avoid one another, except when they *mate* or when a female is raising her cubs.

> *You have probably heard of a pack of dogs, a school of fish, or a herd of horses. But have you heard of a streak of tigers? That's what a group of tigers is called. Although tigers are usually solitary, occasionally a small family group will gather for a short time to cool off in a river or nap in the shade.*

THIS SIBERIAN TIGER HUNTS ON THE EDGE OF A CONIFEROUS FOREST IN RUSSIA.

3
THE LONE HUNTER

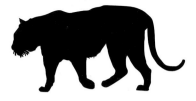

Moving silently through the forest, a tiger hunts alone in the night. It has been several nights since it has had any food, and it is hungry. Through the leaves, the tiger's sharp eyes glimpse a spotted deer raising its head to feed.

Taking one cautious step after another, the tiger draws near its prey. One false step and the

TIGERS LEARN TO STALK AT AN EARLY AGE. HERE, A FOURTEEN-WEEK-OLD WHITE BENGAL TIGER PRACTICES STALKING.

A SIBERIAN TIGER STALKS ITS PREY THROUGH THE WATER.

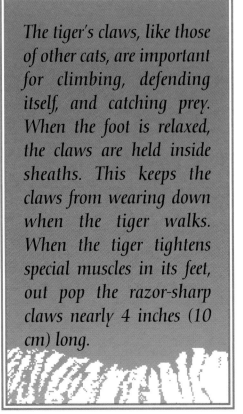

The tiger's claws, like those of other cats, are important for climbing, defending itself, and catching prey. When the foot is relaxed, the claws are held inside sheaths. This keeps the claws from wearing down when the tiger walks. When the tiger tightens special muscles in its feet, out pop the razor-sharp claws nearly 4 inches (10 cm) long.

deer will whistle a warning to others and disappear into the forest. The tiger is patient. It must be. If it does not get close enough to catch its prey in one quick burst of speed, it will go hungry again. Tigers rely on ambush and strength to catch their prey. They are not built for running long distances. As fierce as they seem, tigers miss more than they catch.

Suddenly, the tiger leaps forward, covering 15 feet (5 m) in a single bound. The deer turns—but too late. In the next bound, the tiger grabs the deer between its sharp claws and knocks it to the ground. Immediately, it bites the deer's neck. With its windpipe crushed, the deer suffocates.

The tiger eats its fill right away, gobbling as much as 40 pounds (18 kg) of food. It drags any leftovers into the brush and covers them with leaves to hide them from *scavengers*. When the tiger gets hungry again, it will return for more.

A SIBERIAN TIGER BOUNDS AT ITS PREY.

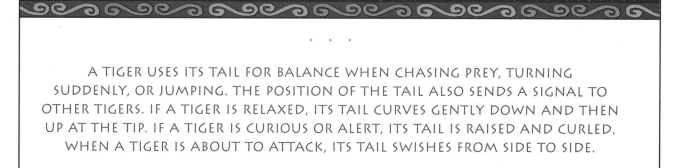

A TIGER USES ITS TAIL FOR BALANCE WHEN CHASING PREY, TURNING SUDDENLY, OR JUMPING. THE POSITION OF THE TAIL ALSO SENDS A SIGNAL TO OTHER TIGERS. IF A TIGER IS RELAXED, ITS TAIL CURVES GENTLY DOWN AND THEN UP AT THE TIP. IF A TIGER IS CURIOUS OR ALERT, ITS TAIL IS RAISED AND CURLED. WHEN A TIGER IS ABOUT TO ATTACK, ITS TAIL SWISHES FROM SIDE TO SIDE.

TIGERS CATCH THEIR PREY WITH A SINGLE BURST OF SPEED.

A SWIFT BITE TO THE NECK WILL KILL THE PREY QUICKLY.

Each tiger has its own area of land called a *territory*. To make sure that other tigers keep away, tigers mark their territory by scratching the bark on tree trunks or by scent marking. To leave scent marks, tigers rub their faces against tree trunks or spray their urine on trees, bushes, grass, and rocks.

The more food and shelter in a territory, the smaller it is. If food and shelter are scarce, a territory might cover

TIGERS MUST EAT AS MUCH OF THEIR KILL AS POSSIBLE. SOMETIMES THEY GO DAYS BETWEEN MEALS.

as many as 400 square miles (103,600 hectares). That's about the size of Los Angeles. Usually, two or three females possess small areas of their own within a male's larger territory.

Tigers search their territories for whatever they can catch. They can bring down animals much larger than themselves. They are also strong swimmers and will hunt in water. Sometimes, they even steal food from crocodiles!

Tigers feed regularly on antelope, deer, and wild pigs. They also eat fish, lizards, snakes, monkeys, birds, squirrels, wild dogs, and even fruit and grass. They have been known to prey on rhinoceros calves, sloth bears, and leopards!

Have you ever seen a cat that loves water? Most cats, including house cats, avoid the water. But tigers are excellent swimmers! They hunt, and even play, in rivers and ponds. When it is hot, they often lie in the water to cool off.

TIGERS SWIM TO COOL OFF, TO CROSS A RIVER, OR EVEN TO CATCH FISH.

4
A TIGER'S LIFE

A female tiger approaches a river. First she drinks. Then she climbs into the water to cool off. She has been wandering her territory for hours, looking for a male with whom to mate. After a short rest, she sets out again. Occasionally she roars softly.

Along the way, she marks her territory, letting the male know she is ready to mate. Her message also tells other females to stay away. If she does meet another female, she will hiss, snarl, and try to chase her away.

Finally, the female hears the deep roar of a male. She trots toward the sound. When the two meet, they approach each other

A FEMALE TIGER LEAVES HER SCENT DURING MATING TIME.

A MALE SIBERIAN TIGER ROARS IN RESPONSE TO A FEMALE'S CALL.

cautiously. The female rolls on the ground and puffs air out of her nose. She is saying that she wants to mate.

Approaching the male, she rubs against him and licks his face. They mate several times over the next few days. After mating, they go their separate ways. The male will not help to raise the young. In fact, females with young avoid other tigers, especially males. Male tigers often kill cubs.

ONCE TOGETHER, MALE AND FEMALE TIGERS WILL SOMETIMES GROWL OR EVEN SWAT AT EACH OTHER BEFORE MATING.

Over the next three–and–a–half months, the female keeps hunting, even when her belly is bulging with the young. She has to. No other tiger will hunt for her. When the time comes, she finds a secret den deep in a thicket or cave. Inside, she gives birth.

The tiger is only one of over four thousand mammals living on Earth today. Mammals are unique among other animals in that they nurse their babies with milk. They also have hair and are warm-blooded. This means their bodies produce their own heat. Most mammals give birth to live young. Only the platypus and echidnas lay eggs.

THIS SIBERIAN TIGER CUB
IS ONLY A FEW DAYS OLD.

A SIBERIAN MOTHER PLAYS WITH HER CUBS OUTSIDE
THEIR DEN.

Her babies—usually two or three—are born blind and helpless. Each weighs about 2 or 3 pounds (1.5 kg). Moments after they are born, the cubs begin to mew.

Within days, the female returns to the hunt. At first, she hunts close to the den, returning often to nurse her cubs. As they get older, the mother leaves the cubs for longer periods.

After two months, the female leads her cubs away from the den. She takes them to a nearby kill to eat meat for the first time. For the next several months, the mother takes the cubs out every day to eat, play, and explore.

When the cubs are about six months old, she takes them on their first hunt. They are clumsy at first, making too much noise and moving at the wrong time. But slowly they learn. In a year or two they will hunt as well as their mother.

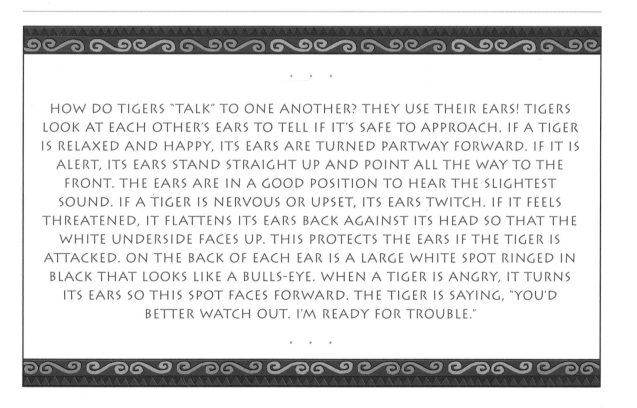

HOW DO TIGERS "TALK" TO ONE ANOTHER? THEY USE THEIR EARS! TIGERS LOOK AT EACH OTHER'S EARS TO TELL IF IT'S SAFE TO APPROACH. IF A TIGER IS RELAXED AND HAPPY, ITS EARS ARE TURNED PARTWAY FORWARD. IF IT IS ALERT, ITS EARS STAND STRAIGHT UP AND POINT ALL THE WAY TO THE FRONT. THE EARS ARE IN A GOOD POSITION TO HEAR THE SLIGHTEST SOUND. IF A TIGER IS NERVOUS OR UPSET, ITS EARS TWITCH. IF IT FEELS THREATENED, IT FLATTENS ITS EARS BACK AGAINST ITS HEAD SO THAT THE WHITE UNDERSIDE FACES UP. THIS PROTECTS THE EARS IF THE TIGER IS ATTACKED. ON THE BACK OF EACH EAR IS A LARGE WHITE SPOT RINGED IN BLACK THAT LOOKS LIKE A BULLS-EYE. WHEN A TIGER IS ANGRY, IT TURNS ITS EARS SO THIS SPOT FACES FORWARD. THE TIGER IS SAYING, "YOU'D BETTER WATCH OUT. I'M READY FOR TROUBLE."

After about a year, the cubs have become more independent. They no longer play together. They hunt on their own. By the age of two or three, the young leave and find a territory of their own.

A young female usually sets up a territory within or next to her mother's. Because of this, neighboring females are often related. They may be daughters, sisters, aunts, or cousins. In most cases, once a female has a territory and mates with a male, she will stay there for the rest of her life. If she dies, another relative will take over. If a larger, stronger female chases her from her territory, she may become a wanderer and never mate again.

A young male, on the other hand, must travel away from his birth area to find a territory. This keeps closely-related tigers from mating with each other. A young male might have to live in a place with fewer trees and game until he is able to take a better territory.

An old male tiger is dying. Stiff and slow, he can no

THESE YOUNG CUBS ARE PLAY-FIGHTING. THE SKILLS THEY LEARN PLAYING WILL HELP THEM DEFEND THEMSELVES WHEN THEY GET OLDER.

longer catch his prey. A young male notices that the old male is no longer marking his territory. Cautiously, the young tiger enters. When he is sure he can chase off the old tiger or when the old tiger dies, he moves in permanently. He will live about fourteen years, ruling his new land, until he, too, is replaced by a younger male.

A YOUNG BENGAL TIGER IN INDIA SEARCHES FOR A TERRITORY OF ITS OWN.

5
BIG CATS IN CRISIS

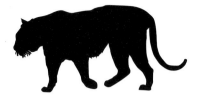

Eighty years ago, there were over 100,000 tigers in the world. Today, there are only five to seven thousand left in the wild and in national parks and nature reserves. Will the world lose the last of its wild tigers?

Three subspecies—the Caspian tiger, the Bali tiger, and the Javan tiger—have died out. Siberian tigers and Sumatran tigers number in the mere hundreds. Only about twenty South China tigers remain. It may be too late for them to recover.

One word can explain why: people. The number of tigers began to shrink well over a hundred years ago, when Europeans settling in Asia became big game hunters. Tigers had little chance against firearms.

A BENGAL TIGER RELAXES IN A PROTECTED AREA OF INDIA.

Hunting tigers was finally outlawed, but *poachers* still kill them. They sell the skins and bones on the *black market*. The skins are made into rugs and wall hangings. The bones have long been used in eastern Asia to make medicines aimed at healing people or at helping them feel younger.

In the meantime, human populations have been growing. People want places to live, farm, and raise their livestock. To do that, they cut down the forests where tigers live. They kill the animals that tigers eat. Then when tigers get hungry, they kill farm animals and sometimes even people. To protect their farm animals, people kill tigers.

Tigers will not survive unless people work hard to save them. Many efforts have already been made to protect tigers. Some people who make traditional medicines are looking for substitutes for tiger bones. Others are trying to save the forests. These forests, besides being home to tigers and other wild animals, are an important part of the earth's environment.

In some areas, tourists come to see tigers in the wild. Local people make a living as guides for tourists. In a

WHEN HUNTING, PEOPLE ATTACH MASKS TO THE BACKS OF THEIR HEADS TO FOOL TIGERS. TIGERS WILL NOT ATTACK IF THEY CAN SEE A PERSON'S FACE.

IN INDIA, TERRITORY THAT TIGERS ONCE ROAMED HAS BEEN TURNED INTO FARMLAND TO PROVIDE FOOD FOR THE GROWING HUMAN POPULATION.

41

few places, the tiger is now making a small comeback.

If people around the world keep working together, the tiger just might make it. But we need to act now; its time is running out.

SOME LAND, SUCH AS THE MADHYA PRADESH TIGER RESERVE IN INDIA, SHOWN HERE, HAS BEEN SET ASIDE ESPECIALLY FOR TIGERS.

THESE TOURISTS ARE ON A TIGER SAFARI IN RANTAMBOR, INDIA.

black market: The illegal buying and selling of goods.

camouflage: A disguise or false appearance that helps an animal blend into its surroundings.

coniferous: A tree that bears cones, such as a pine or spruce.

deciduous: A tree that loses its leaves each year.

evergreen: A tree whose leaves stay green year-round.

mate: To join as a pair in order to produce young.

poacher: A person who hunts or fishes illegally.

predator: An animal that lives by killing and eating other animals.

prey: An animal hunted for food by another animal.

scavenger: An animal that feeds on the kill of another animal.

species: A kind of animal with similar features that is able to reproduce.

subspecies: A group within a species of plant or animal that lives in a particular area. Bengal tigers and Sumatran tigers are two sub-species of tigers.

territory: An area chosen by an animal or group of animals as its own.

tropical: of, in, or like the tropics.

tropics: The region of Earth just north and south of the equator that is noted for its hot, wet climate and thick forests.

BOOKS

Barnes, Simon. *Tiger!* New York: St. Martin's Press, 1994.

Burton, Maurice and Robert. *Encyclopedia of Mammals.* London: Octopus Books, 1975.

Harman, Amanda. *Tigers.* Endangered! Series. Tarrytown, NY: Marshall Cavendish, 1996.

Morris, Desmond. *Cat World: A Feline Encyclopedia.* New York: Penguin, 1997.

National Geographic Book of Mammals. Volume Two. Washington, DC: National Geographic Society, 1981.

Wexo, John. *Big Cats.* Poway, CA: Zoobooks/Wildlife Education; 1997.

WEBSITES

Tiger Information Center
www.5tigers.org

World Wildlife Fund
www.panda.org

Cyber Tiger
www.nationalgeographic.com/tigers

Susan Schafer is a writer and science teacher who enjoys sharing her love for animals with others. She has written a number of books about animals, including *Turtles* and *Lizards* in the Marshall Cavendish Perfect Pets series. She lives on a ranch outside of San Luis Obispo, California, where she is occasionally blessed with the sighting of a mountain lion.

INDEX

Page numbers for photos are in **boldface**.